Singily Skipping along

story by
Sheree Fitch

art by
Deanne Fitzpatrick

NIMBUS
PUBLISHING

Nimbus Publishing Limited
3731 Mackintosh St, Halifax, NS B3K 5A5
(902) 455-4286 nimbus.ca

Printed and bound in China

Author photo: Kate Inglis
Illustrator photo: Lorna Davis
Design: Jenn Embree
NB1063

Library and Archives Canada Cataloguing in Publication

Fitch, Sheree, author
Singily skipping along / story by Sheree Fitch ; art by
Deanne Fitzpatrick.
    A poem.
    ISBN 978-1-77108-091-0 (bound)

I. Fitzpatrick, Deanne, illustrator II. Title.

PS8561.I86S46 2013   jC811'.54   C2013-903434-X

Nimbus Publishing acknowledges the financial support for its publishing activities from the Government of Canada through the Canada Book Fund (CBF) and the Canada Council for the Arts, and from the Province of Nova Scotia through the Department of Communities, Culture and Heritage.

For Shirley Craft and all the Early Childhood Educators who singily skip along and bring books to life.
—S. F.

For Mikhial and Adele, may you be and feel all that you can.
—D. F.

This is a tree

I am a tree

I am a maple tree

Dancing in wind.

This is a drum

I am a drum

I am a-thumpety

Drumming a song.

This is a stone

I am a stone

I am a-hushily

Breathing in

light.

This is a lake

I am a duck

I am a-quackily

Splash-happy

day.

This is a star

I am the moon

I am a shiningly

Circle of round.

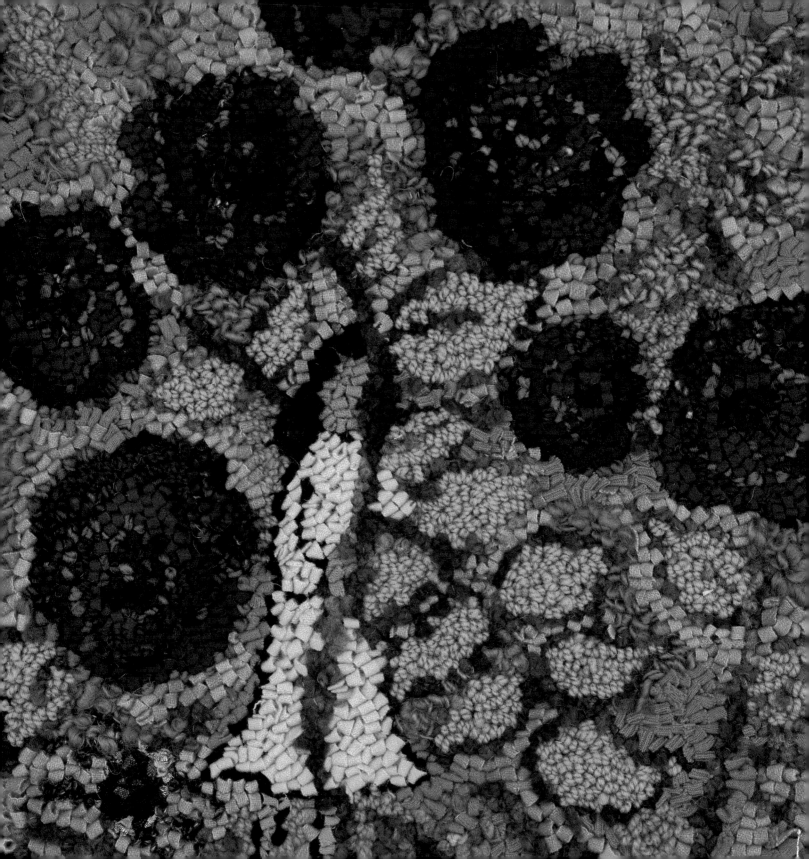

This is a rose

        I am a thorn

I am a-prickly

        Stinging like me

This is a spider

        I am a fly

I am a-stickily

        Stuck like me

This is the cheese

I am a mouse

I am a squeakily

Nibbling kiss.

This is a sea

I am a whale

I am a **Smilingly**

Wide-open hug.

This is the wind

I am a leaf

I am a *flutter-by*

Butterfly wish.

This is an apple

I am a worm

I am *a-squirmily*

Warming the ground.

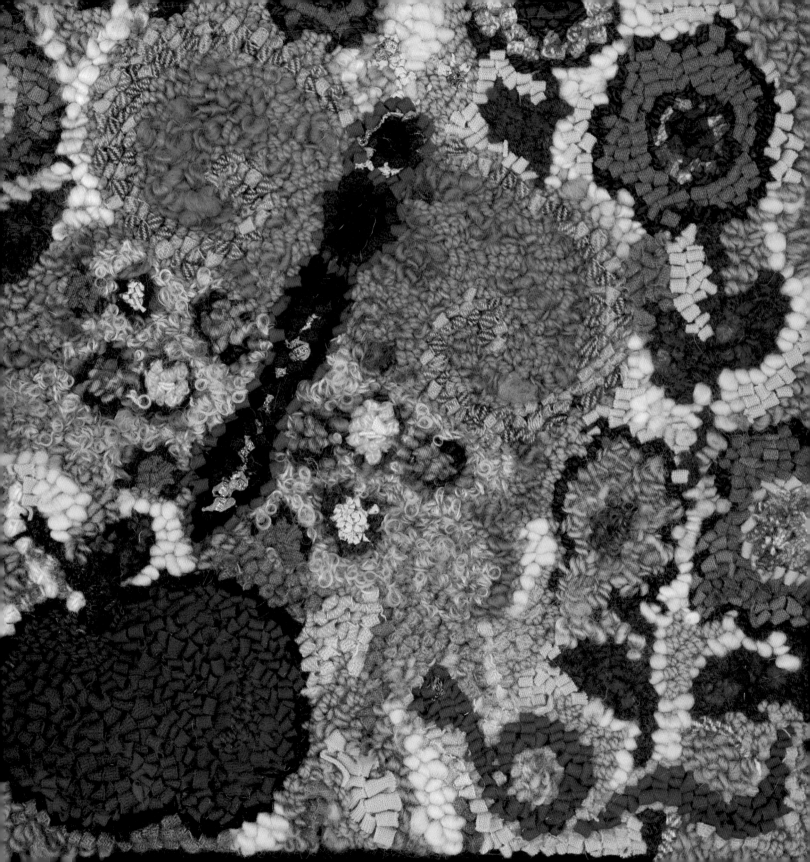

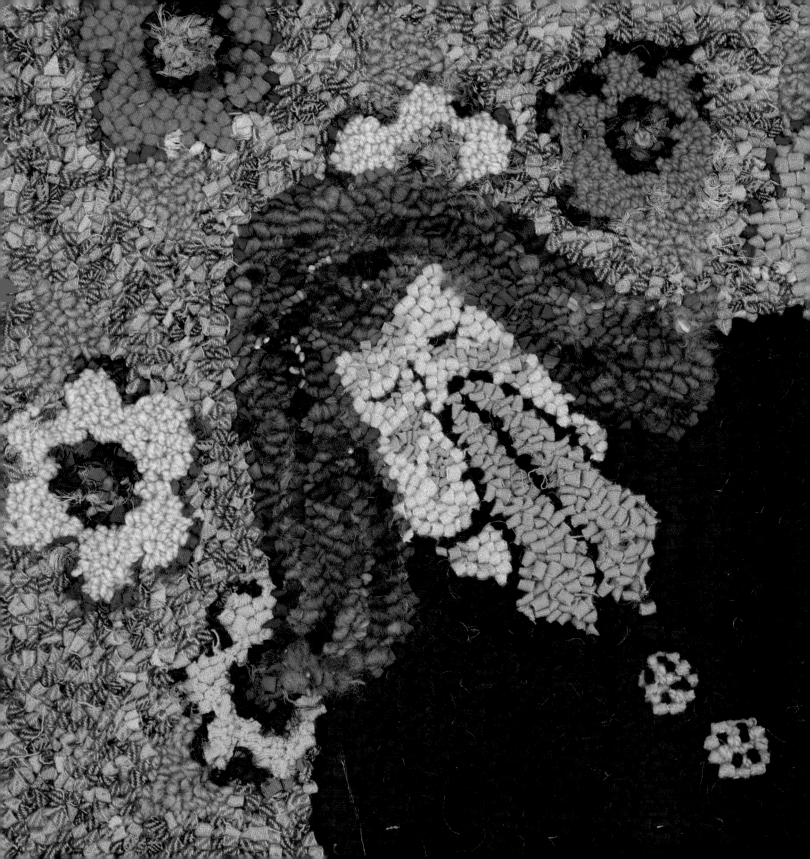

This is a face

I am a nose

There's no other itchily

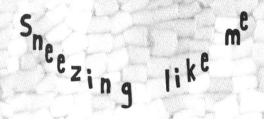

This is a foot

I am the toes

There's no other

tickle-ish

Stinkle like me

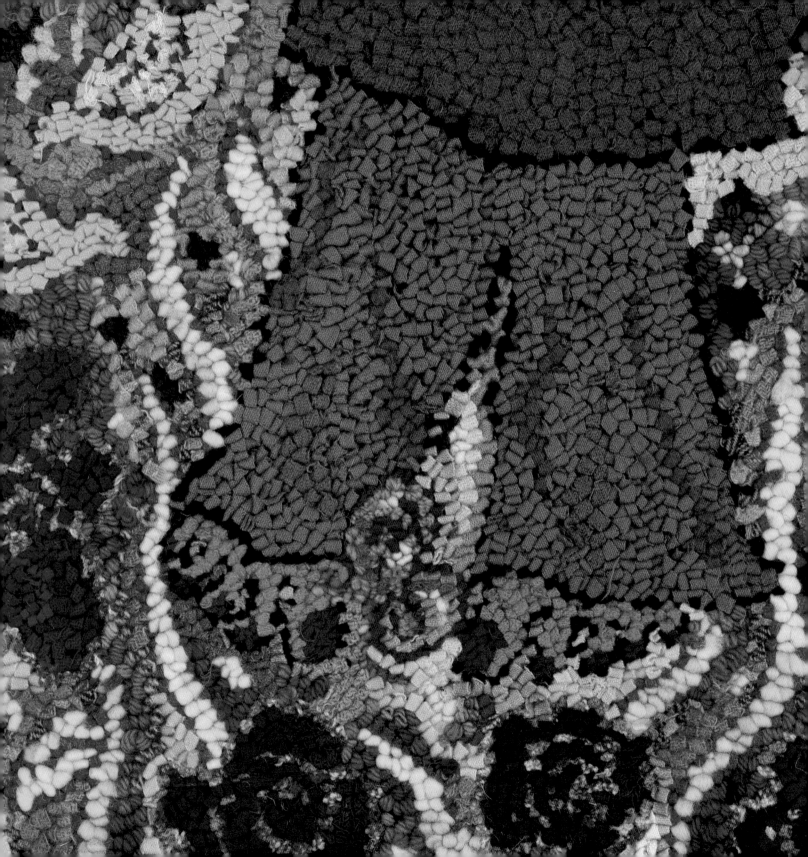

This is the sun

I am a cloud

There's no other shadow

As sparkly as mine

This is a day

I am a song

There's no other singily

skipping along.

This is a dad

I am a girl

There's no other hand

As **warm** as mine

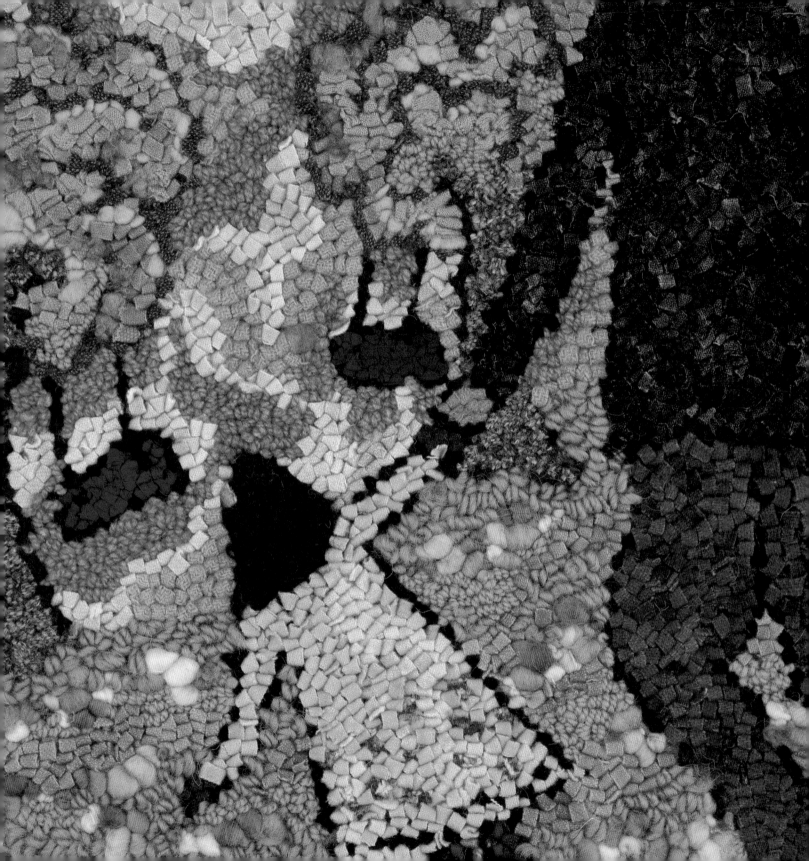

This is a mom

I am a boy

There's no other *huggily*

Arms like yours

There's no other you like you

There's no other me like me

Quackily stickily

squeakily squirmily

tickley prickly

huggily happily

Singily skipping along!